SHEARSMAN

107 & 108

SUMMER 2016

EDITOR
TONY FRAZER

This issue is dedicated to the memory of

CHRISTOPHER MIDDLETON

(b. Truro, 10 June 1926;
d. Austin, TX, 29 November 2015)

Shearsman magazine is published in the United Kingdom by
Shearsman Books Ltd
50 Westons Hill Drive | Emersons Green | BRISTOL BS16 7DF

Registered office: 30-31 St James Place, Mangotsfield, Bristol BS16 9JB
(this address not for correspondence)

www. shearsman.com

ISBN 978-1-84861-478-9
ISSN 0260-8049

Subscriptions and single copies

Current subscriptions—covering two double-issues, with an average length of
108 pages—cost £16 for delivery to U.K. addresses, £18 for the rest of Europe
(including the Republic of Ireland), and £21 for the rest of the world. Longer sub-
scriptions may be had for a pro-rata higher payment. North American customers
will find that buying single copies from online retailers in the U.S.A. will often be
cheaper than subscribing. This is because airmail postage rates in the U.K. have
risen rapidly, whereas copies of the magazine are printed in the U.S.A. to meet
demand from online retailers there, and thus avoid the transatlantic mail.

Back issues from n° 63 onwards (uniform with this issue) cost £8.95 / $16 through
retail outlets. Single copies can be ordered for £8.95 direct from the press, post-free
in the U.K., through the Shearsman Books online store, or from any bookshop.
Issues of the previous pamphlet-style version of the magazine, from
n° 1 to n° 62, may be had for £3 each, direct from the press, where copies are
still available, but contact us for a quote for a full, or partial, run.

Submissions

Shearsman operates a submissions-window system, whereby submissions are only
accepted during the months of March and September, when selections are
made for the October and April issues, respectively. Submissions may be sent
by mail or email, but email attachments—other than PDFs—are not accepted.
We aim to respond within 3 months of the window's closure.

Acknowledgements

'Der Gärtner sät Rasen ins Unkraut', 'Bald ist der Mai vorbei', 'Nur abgedunkelt',
'Cutty Sark', 'Nach Wörtern Suchen' & 'Kartographien' from: Günter Eich:
Sämtliche Gedichte © Suhrkamp Verlag, 2007; with the friendly permission of
Suhrkamp Verlag Berlin. 'Europa' by Marie-Luise Kaschnitz is likewise printed
here by permission of Suhrkamp Verlag Berlin.

Contents

Harry Guest

Alteration

Wishing at times things wouldn't change

> *these leaves to hold their gold and pools*
> *to guard a wayward cloud stained by*
> *a falling sun unmoved its curves*
> *unfretted all the tones between*
> *electric scarlet and a smear*
> *of almost green to catch before*
> *their fading disappoints to greys*
> *eventual dark like foliage*
> *that crackled underfoot turned brown*
> *then to no colour only slush*
> *a nuisance broomed away as both*
> *the dying and the dyeing lie*
> *in movement paradoxically.*

> *Time lingers sometimes with the dusk*
> *at hand to shroud those boughs against*
> *the sky once any suns have left*
> *a glowing backdrop to their fate*
> *replaced perhaps by rain*

— is wrong —
or even childish. Recognition, life
from birth past death, growth, fever, failure, all
is change brought forward for the best
though often vice versa, worse
than hope had been so sure about.
A transitory fact is such
you know each lived-in moment won't
survive except in files, cold archives, vaults,
and they too are a waiting prey
or likelihood. Worms, lightning, flood,
moths, conflagration, every threat

4

from earth, fire, water, even air
when hurricanes are imminent,
cascades which wear away the very rock
that made them so impressive or
pollution

         (Niikuni's so
         meticulously concrete print
         of kanji'd pus — one small space only on
         the centre of those seas still holds
         pure water).

                Hard to learn again
how all is temporary, will
be lost, destroyed or just not there
now. If we rot, towns fall, birds beasts
fish insects one by one become
a sad guess like a dinosaur
or dodo how can we regret
the exit of a sunset, loss
of petals and the daily drift
to nothing of the details in
those photos we took long ago.
You can't stop music like an act
caught by some cunning camera of
three leaping dancers in mid-air,
the sword about to win the duel
immobile near the soon to be
struck heart that goes on throbbing till
the movie moves again and then
no more. So symphonies switched off
aren't there, there's nothing to assess
like the iced smile or silent scream.
It's not the question of a note
sounding for ever. Sound has gone.
The flow of intricate response
from flute to cello, sharp to flat,
now nowhere like the absence of
touch, hearing, taste, sight, odours like
dismay, joy, carelessness and love.

All must go on and fade or stay
in place for languished moments, know
what's mourned in time and then replaced
by need or apathy, get thrilled
by novelties which never last
forgotten sooner than the start
of autumn when all will go on
to snow and bleak sterility
and then to spring and yet again
to spring so better shrug, ignore,
walk out in rain and back in hail,
deny, remember wrongly, dream,
plant hyacinths, yawn, weep, sketch out
another novel, squander, fail
to pray, recover, understand,
play Mozart clumsily and wish
in vain things didn't change until

Alexandra Sashe

Ode to Spring

White councils
of the season

sun-bleached days
    before the harvest.

Rooms enfold with a static confidence
afternoon hours lived with windows'
immaculate lungs, umbilical sunlight.

An angel draws upon the wall
    words eternally pregnant with silence :

unspoken, with clasped hands,
we lean against his wings.

A newly reborn hour
bequeaths us its renatal clothes.
                We exit the clock and slough
                our names and shadows.

                The angel retraces upon the sky
                        our outlines
                        with chalk.

Lenten

Spring transcends with a quiet step
its thaw, – with an amorous hand
breaks the mirrors.

Its ardour leaves unstirred the surface
of spring water, smooth the surface
made of cloth, of virgin paper,
of stained porcelain.

The Spring justifies him who receives it
with cupped hands,
with open arms,
with naked face
and uncovered shoulders ;
with palm branches
    and mute mute
        solitary walks
up and down the hill.

of Evolution

This tree, departed from its species,
all ashes sweeper.

in our secret, we grow
    skin and bark,
        rootlessful,
sacri- and *sancti-*
        -fied
kernels and bones,
    sky- and heaven-
        wards.

(We part and depart,
    abnegate and negate
        ourselves,
        taking turns,
in the deciduous season,
    florescence season,

dispelling our selves,
spelling
            the selves away,
upholding each other – for bridges –
slenderly, over each winter)

in our secret
we are in light :
a spacious room,
a timeless hour.

Here, you have grown an olive branch.
Here, I am seeing the dove in.

of Genealogy

ink and paper
cross and plough

                              ripening fruits,
                              Vôtres

les miens : arms
too light to fly
too light to sink
too blind to count
too open to carry
too bare
        to bear a name.

An illegitimate language,
                        mine,
discalced, orphan and hermit.

a daily ultimate sip
of thirst,
the Thebaid purpose
                  and reflex.

A grain of sand
covering miles of legends.
A drop of water capsizing the Babel vessel.
Illegitimate language,–
a bridge and a walk
     over the circuits.

Each verbal unit
pronounced = denounced :

a narrow path
  towards Adoption.

a Spring Song

[earthly]

A vernal sun occupies my place,
a solitary demi-seasonal
mezzo-soprano whisper.

Elided vowels make their way back
at a quiet pace.

The plane tree will shed in retrospect
over the square
abandoned and disavowed property of
the ante-renatal words :

husks and petals
in heartfuls   in handfuls.

a Spring Song

[a Song for Elias]

Water well   sun well
prophetic resistance
to stone and arrow
    to tongues
        of fire
distilling the souls upwards
    to heaven via
aqueducts, logs, bows.

The chariot built
    in a simple syntactic order.
The chant, of a circular verbal matter.

Prophets sow themselves into the ploughed soil,
and burn forth
in heartfuls   in handfuls.

Alan Wall

The Posthumous Reflections of Sir John Soane

1 13 Lincoln's Inn Fields

Observe this morning's luminous *étude*:
how godhead enters
man's diminutive stone wigwam.
Molten gold. Zeus impregnating
Danaë's brazen tower.

Alone once more I light a fire
kindled from sundry owl-eyes
crystal tears from Pliny's crocodiles
one lizard tongue, its wreath of ribboned flame
a rainbow dancing. [1]

---

[1] 13 Lincoln's Inn Fields in London was once the home of Sir John Soane (1753 –1837), and is now his museum. Soane, the most inventive architect of his day, had a lifelong obsession with the interior effects of light, and he could be equally unexpected in his treatment of exteriors. The loggia of Number 13 is made of Portland Stone, and inserted into it are four corbel stones, dating from the fourteenth century, taken from Westminster Hall. This loggia displays the incised lines which Soane employed to indicate pilasters and columns, instead of reproducing them in three dimensions, once they had retained no structural purpose. The radical modernity of these incised lines, together with the antiquity of the corbel stones, displays Soane's genius at a glance: the present must keep hold of the past, and the past is ever-dependent on the present for its presentation and survival. Nothing could better summarise Soane's architectural philosophy. The kindling items listed here are imaginary, but are in fact no stranger than many of the objects to be discovered in the basement of 13 Lincoln's Inn Fields.

2 Chiaroscuro

Light was ever my study
its high enchantments
grading down to shadowed rest.
How Helios caresses his brief creatures
for a day (we are ephemera, no more)
before arriving with one hot kiss
to sign us off.
A holy breath that smells of asphodel
spearmint
the faintest hint of methylated spirit.

The canopy in my Breakfast Room
suspends from nothing visible
so light arrives from everywhere and nowhere.
Each time an eggshell cracks
hosts of angels chant masonic halleluiahs.

Each lunette His peephole. [2]

---

[2] Soane was a mason in all possible senses. His father had been a bricklayer. The boy learned the craft of making buildings from the material foundations upwards, as masons in antiquity reportedly did too. In 1813 he himself was initiated as a Freemason, and had a portrait painted of himself in full Masonic dress. He went on to design the Masonic Hall on Great Queen Street. And in his obsession with the effects of light, he was reflecting the central Masonic belief that God, as architect of the universe, spoke through light, since He Himself could never see a shadow. Freemasonry can be seen as the natural religion of the Enlightenment, its emblems appear on the title page of the *Encyclopédie*, and so it is appropriate that the luminous syllable at the heart of that word Enlightenment became Soane's lifelong study. Each mausoleum he devised is intended to be shrouded in light. He himself translated Le Camus de Mézières' book *The Genius of Architecture, or the Analogy of that Art with our Sensations*. In that work Le Camus expounds his doctrine of *lumière mystérieuse*.

3 Amanuensis

Out of the sepulchral cave
a cult man comes, dressed in shadows
having gleaned the secrets of the dead.
Ready to survey the tumulus
check that its burial ship is caulked and tarred
Arthur once more ready for his journey.

The day Joe Gandy arrives in heaven
he'll promptly paint the place in ruins
as eternal sunset fractures to a million lucid shards.
Then watch our man present his panorama to the seraphim
waive any bill in lieu of future kindnesses
doubtless to be given him in Paradise.

I only hope they take him at his word
a good man destined for a dark asylum
whose incomparable eye will never
see the good clear day again.

Joe Gandy, Patmos John to me
limner of my curious Apocalypse
its megaliths and microliths.

Mine the shining city on the hill. [3]

[3] Joseph Gandy (1771-1843) effectively became John Soane's painter. He depicted not merely the edifices Soane was planning to have built, but also the ones that never would be built. Never could be built. Vast cities on imaginary hills. Buildings that achieve their only life on Gandy's canvases. Regarded in his day as a failed architect, altogether too awkward professionally ever to succeed, and therefore obliged to hang on to Soane's coat-tails, he is now thought to be a genius of a curious and rare nature: he could imagine into being architectural scenes of such grandeur of spirit that it seems as if they really must have been built; built in the only place his contemporary William Blake believed anything ever could be permanently built – in the vast labyrinth of the imagination. His vision of Merlin's sepulchre, or of a Pandemonium taken out of Milton, inhabit a topographic world of their own.

He and Soane shared a land of vision, a terrain midway between the antique ruin and the modern dream. If the obverse of the Enlightenment world was Palladian design with its lucid structures of symmetry, white stucco walls encasing shining interiors, there was always a reverse to this vision of logic and reason. Many buildings of the time employ exaggerated rustication in their basement storeys, as though acknowledging all the roughness, the incommensurable chaos that could never be translated to exposition and justice. This was the age of misshapen hermitages, hidden away in the grounds of grand estates. Sometimes hermits were actually employed to fill them, as though Poor Tom were still hidden away in his hovel, awaiting the arrival of the demented king. Piranesi's *Carceri* provided glooms deep enough for the abyssal opium journeyings of a De Quincey – and both Gandy and Soane were devoted to Piranesi. They both contemplated mausoleums so beautiful no corpse would ever decompose inside them. They saw Rome in ruins; in the distance oriental monuments of unimaginable grandeur. The whole suffused with the ambience of a cosmic twilight. Like John Martin, Gandy created palaces with smoke emitting from them, potent enough to occlude the sky. This was after all the age of industry and revolution. Something else to be made out on the horizon. The eyes of the great Mason had to squinny sometimes, in order to retain their focus. Gandy's wits finally came astray, and he ended his life in an asylum in Plympton. There is a tradition that King Arthur sleeps in the Welsh hills, but since he is *rex quondam rexque futurus*, he will awake one day and return in glory.

4 Inventory

Item:
One terracotta of Aeneas
carrying Anchises out of burning Troy
upon his shoulders.
Were it my son George
he'd throw me back
into the Trojan flames
and grin.

Into his mother's womb
I injected treachery
for which I am
repaid in kind, each day.
Repaid most handsomely. [4]

---

[4] This might be the saddest part of the whole story, sadder even than the destruction of his Bank of England in 1925, for this was the familial ruin that he had to live with daily. The son, one of two, was called George. Soane had dreamed that this boy would become a great architect like his father. He even built ruins for him at Pitzhanger Manor over in Ealing, so as to give the lad something to get his teeth into. But George preferred chewing on other things entirely. If he inherited one thing from his old man it was neither his architectural flair nor his ability for such mighty toil, but that saddest of all bequests: *ressentiment*. Both father and son had a genius for this corroding faculty, the acid solvent of the soul, but only the son actually made it into a career. For years, as Mrs Soane received the peevish, ill-tempered and abusive letters from her offspring, ceaselessly riddled with demands for money, money, and yet more money, payment for a life with no real purpose but parasitism and revenge, she hid them from her husband, knowing the fury they would provoke in him. In the *Champion* a two-part article was published, *The Present Low State of the Arts in England and more particularly of Architecture*. Soane's work was singled out for a venomous attack. It was soon established that the anonymous piece was actually the work of Soane's younger son, and Mrs Soane did not long survive the revelation. George was ultimately imprisoned for fraud. He was later to try to prevent the Act of Parliament which facilitated the endowment of his father's museum, believing the money concerned should go to him instead. When Soane invented the Monk's Parlour at Lincoln's Inn Fields, he also invented the disconsolate eremite who had seemingly lived down there among his memories of the earthly life and thwarted love. *Padre Giovanni* he called him. Father John. Father John had been so tormented by the world that he had left it behind for a life of meditation and prayer. One senses that John Soane, the father, not infrequently envied his own creation.

5 Lachrimae rerum

Two glass lachrymatories I purchased
at the Yarnold Sale of 1825
vanished in the lists of 1837
(ah how the tears of yesteryear
gain antique lustre
with every day that passes)
stolen perhaps by one
who scarce knew how to cry himself.

I think I know his name.

An incubus riding the corpse of my elevations. [5]

---

[5] All ages have their intellectual clichés. One of ours is the Oedipus Complex. So awful were relations between father and son that we might even be tempted to invoke it, but there was no such notion available for either of them to invoke at the time. Soane would have been entirely baffled by any such reference to Oedipus, who was called upon then as a solver of riddles. As in Ben Jonson's line from *Sejanus*: 'I am not Oedipus inough, To vnderstand this Sphynx.' The nearest usage to a medical notion would have been *oedipodic*, signifying a swollen foot. The infant Oedipus had had his ankles pierced, so as to facilitate his death from exposure. Even as late as 1928, when the first full edition of the OED appeared, there was no reference to *oedipal* in its Freudian sense. How times change. Curious, is it not, the tradition of preserving someone's tears in tiny receptacles? Soane's buildings all tended to be reduced soon enough to rubble. And so his elevations were levelled. Only the groundplan remained. Lines incised on a grey metal plate.

6 Palaeontology: its records

What do we know of seeing
who barely open our eyes
before they close once more?
Now look hard at this trilobite
nestling in my palm so tranquilly.
Calcite eyes. Calcium Carbonate.
Same stuff made the white cliffs of Dover.

So much white powder
since those once living are now dead.
After millions of years
commanding the ocean floor.

He fashions fossils
(the Great Mason)
as I shape ruins:
our only true and lasting gift to time. [6]

---

[6] Soane lived on into the great age of fossil diagnosis. Fossils had for centuries been employed to exemplify, back up or clinch whatever version of life, cosmology and creation the displayer elected to project. In the *Wunderkammer*, they were even exhibited as sinister creations from the left hand of God, products of the vital energy of earth. And sometimes they were the Satanic exercises that took place under cover of darkness, when no one was looking. But some had already spotted the living form in the petrified remains. Leonardo and Robert Hooke were both in no doubt what these fossils represented. And throughout the eighteenth century, palaeontology proceeded apace. Riddling out the meaning of those bones soon transmuted antiquarianism into science. This process could be haphazard: Cuvier's readings of the ancient skeletons placed before him, often lifted from the gypsum quarries of Montmartre, were hampered by his belief in the Biblical Flood, and the immutability of species. But in countless publications, like the Transactions of the Royal Society, the fossils were being analysed, a sense of the past life of the planet was being attempted. Geomorphology and stratigraphy proceeded apace. The trilobite was one of the most successful species that has ever lived. It lasted for hundreds of millions of years, then simply disappeared in one of the great extinctions. All that was left were fossils; time's ruins. Soane's obsession with ruins was once more vindicated. He had even built his own. And Gandy painted the ones still to come. In this vision, the ruin is our ultimate destination.

7 Climatic

Bent by disappointment and the English cold
even the joints of my thought grow rigid
ferrules with hellebores of frost blossoming upon them.

Hurrying down this parquet corridor
towards my lecture at the RA
I hear shadowed footsteps clattering back towards me
old bones wielded by some ancient vaudevillian.
And resolve to try a smile today
by way of prelude to my mighty theme.
Went down like the skeleton's grin in my Crypt.

For true lightness of heart
my dearest remarked to me one evening
you lack genius, John.

They never did ask me to design a music hall.
(I might well have based it on the Colosseum.)
Nor any place of manufacture for the current metalware. [7]

---

[7] Humour, sadly, was not Soane's strong point. Nor was equable fortitude. As his biographer Dorothy Stroud puts it: 'A sad flaw in Soane's character was his inability to weigh his misfortunes against his blessings.' All his joy went into his buildings and designs. He conceived churches and houses, banks and privy chambers, a great many palaces and temples that were never built, and funerary structures, cenotaphs and mausoleums. The one at Dulwich still stands, as does the one he built for his own family, in what was once St Giles's Burial Ground and is now St Pancras Gardens. First he put his wife in it, then he followed her there himself. These days it constitutes a sad little island surrounded by ceaseless traffic. Even Gandy never dreamed what species of mill Soane might have devised, given the opportunity. A place, presumably, where Samson might have toiled, surrounded by time's other slaves.

8 Pastoral

A glazier's spider spun my fanlight
lead instead of gossamer
in its busy little gut.
Back then remember a wealthy man
could move a whole village
treating it as nothing but an awkward barn.
Dark mutterings in smoky taverns.
Rumours of revolution.

A land of ornamental parks and crescents
lakesides where a sundial compassed
shadows over manicured lawns
filtering out
so many spendthrift hours.

Where a peasant boy might easily have played his oaten flute
but didn't. [8]

---

[8] The pastoral mode is a curious one. It is a lament for a form of life that never existed in the first place. And the landscaped garden is a physical allusion to a place that never was. We might call it Eden. Inside a *hortus conclusus* the walls remain for ever unbreached, announcing the blessed tidings: *We have not yet fallen.* Even the apple has not managed to drop to the ground. It is doubtless awaiting that day in 1666 in Lincolnshire, when a young man named Isaac, away from Cambridge that summer because of the plague, can observe its descent, and start to ponder the genuine gravity of our situation. Isaac was the only young man in Lincolnshire that day who had the genius not to know something. All the others knew why the apple fell to the ground, since that is simply what apples do – always did and always will. Newton didn't know, and so kept asking the question, and that's why he went on to write *Principia Mathematica*, while the others simply sold the apples. It was a deep suspicion of pastoral that led to Samuel Johnson's criticism of Milton's *Lycidas*. The artificiality of the form, Johnson suggested, disguised an artificiality of feeling. Milton did not in truth have any genuine feelings about Edward King, and so he cast them both as ancient shepherds. And when the pastoral mode saw fit to reconfigure a whole landscape, then it paid to be one of the reconfigurers, rather than the reconfigured.

9 Capriccio

Of all capricci ever painted
none matched Gandy's
for their ruined splendour.

My plans for London
as a classic capital
(vaster than anything devised by Wren
let alone Augustus
or even Augustus Welby Northmore Pugin)
ruined utterly
laid bare at last, shards for archaeologists
and elegiac poets.

The world's most marvellous city
conceived by Yours Truly
reduced from elevation to groundplan
before a single stone was laid.
(My epitaph, it seems. This mason's final lettered stonework.)

The Bank of England ravaged.
Not ruins, some said, but a cutaway axonometric.

Stay with the first perception here. I always do.
Posterity: its sledgehammer. [9]

---

[9] Gandy took to painting Soane's buildings in ruins, often before they had even been built. Thus was the nemesis of time anticipated, before the hour had been announced, or the clock even wound. Soane knew precisely what was coming. On the whole he has been proven right. It was some years yet before the Second Law of Thermodynamics would be formulated, but the entropic principle is built into everything the architect conceived. Those corbel stones in the loggia of 13 Lincoln's Inn Fields had announced themselves as *memento mori*, architecturally speaking.

10 Belzoni Sarcophagus

In Eleusis
flashes of light in the dark
purified the occluded vessels of their bodies.

March, 1825.
The year before I bought Seti's sarcophagus
salvaged from the great necropolis at Thebes.

A three-day reception down in my sepulchral Crypt.
A hundred extra lamps and candelabra
brought in for the purpose from William Collins.
A burial without a body. Discarnate anamnesis.
Lights shone through the tomb's translucent aragonite.
Never had I felt more at home
I who have been much possessed by death
at home here and abroad.

Pointed my guests to the highlights
of all this *lumière mystérieuse*
as wineglasses tinkled and flashed
in a waxing murk of London's evening.
Reproductions of Mausolos
a tomb at Palmyra
furnished with gifts enough
to facilitate arrival in the world we still imagine
the one to come.
Small skeletons among potsherds
a polished round table
on which a single skull was placed.
Its hollow gaze darkedly focused
to return your own with interest.

Joe's paintings. Piranesi too.
Met him back in '78
shortly before the old fellow's death.
His copper engravings of the antiquities of Rome
enchanted me then. Still do.

Our chronicle fragments
little clusters of bric-à-brac
clutched here in an act of loving desperation.
A miniature of the Temple of Vesta at Tivoli.
On the sarcophagus, hieroglyphs cover the whole surface.
Seti no longer to be found within.
Only light remains
Snuffed soon enough.

Almost thought to see him
striding through the Crypt
bestowing his halleluiahs
demanding his grog
in Egyptian.
A posthumous
Pharaonic tipple for this strolling revenant. [10]

---

[10] With enormous ritual and care, we bury the dead. Then with equal fastidious-
ness, once a few centuries or millennia have elapsed, we dig them all up again. Even
the mighty kings we disinter, as though Yorick sprang from the earth for one last
grin, one last grimace, one final exposure. Wherever we let human beings lie where
they drop (as in the Warsaw Ghetto) civilization has been abandoned. For a while,
with sky burials, we transported the deceased to the highest points and then left
them there, so that the heavens might consume them, along with any local raptors.
The rich have always tended to construct elaborate antechambers for their post-
mortem journeyings, whether in the form of pyramids, or the stone tabernacles
in Highgate Cemetery. The explorer Richard Burton's widow built him a massive
stone tent in a graveyard in Mortlake. For months after his death, séances were
held there to summon his spirit, but Burton it seems was already off encountering
unknown vistas, and was too busy to reply. Nomadic in death as in life.

11

Here was a rehearsal, no mistake.
For the curious among you
death can indeed be thus: *Son et Lumière*
without the *Son*.

And my poor Joe
finest artist of the kingdom of Thanatos.

The location of his grave unknown still to this day. [11]

---

[11] What has enlightened thought to do with death? Emperor Joseph II of Vienna
tried to make the whole matter more practicable by introducing re-usable coffins,
thus sparing both effort and expense, and facilitating the optimum decomposition
of the body, which a coffin inevitably retards. It never caught on, not even amongst
the poor, who remained fixedly devoted to a religious sense of awe when con-
fronted with the mortality of their loved ones. One might even call it superstition.
However bright our lamps, it seems, an ultimate dark awaits us. Alexander Pope
acknowledged this at the end of his life:

> Lo! Thy dread Empire, CHAOS! is restored;
> Light dies before thy uncreating word:
> Thy hand, great Anarch! lets the curtain fall;
> And Universal Darkness buries All.

This is the midnight of the sublime. This is the tomb of all meanings. Soane never
blinked long enough to lose sight of it. But for him the light shone in the darkness,
all the way back from Regency England to the Pharaoh, and the darkness compre-
hended it not, not now and not then. How Soane must have smiled as that luminous
little syllable at the heart of the word Enlightenment shone out so clearly through
occluding millennia. According to the calculations of the time, the speed of light
was remarkably close to our present estimations, and certainly speedy enough to
overtake the funeral cortège. If you travel at the speed of light then history stands
still. This is the ambition of all poetry, whether made out of words or stone.

12

My greatest wish: to build the smallest
monastery yet constructed
then disappear inside it
like scotch mist.
An eremitic sole possessor
commanding graffiti and the incised rune
to show the mason of this world
inscribing his *signa* in stone.
A mason's chisel's his pen.
Like Wu Tao-tzu in the Tang Dynasty
who completed his mural
clapped both hands once
then stepped through the temple gates he so recently painted
and was never seen again.
Who then would trace
a single emblem of my disappearance? [12]

---

[12] Soane was obsessed by the symbolism buildings displayed. Symbols carved in the tympanum of the human sensibility were proclamations of what Wittgenstein call 'a form of life'. Such systems do not necessarily die with the original systems that generated them. Soane was much preoccupied with snake symbolism. On his own tomb he contrived a stone ouroboros, a snake swallowing its own tail. Emblem of eternity and endless renewal. The present swallows the past, as the future will swallow the present, as the loggia at Lincoln's Inn Fields contained the corbel stones that could never have imagined such a future for themselves. Old symbols find new life, new meaning. They resurrect through allegory and interpretation. So Francis Bacon saw in Pan an allegory of Nature; so Freud (a great admirer of Bacon) saw in Oedipus an allegory of murderous infantile desire. What troubled Soane was not such vivifying acts of translation but the retention of ancient symbols as mere ballast, part of the architectural heritage when it has become a dead language. What did the Roman eagle mean by the time it arrived north of Hadrian's Wall? On the other hand, any set of symbols can start to shine brightly once more, if they discover themselves formed into a novel constellation. Let Psyche be intellectual inquiry, however devoted, bringing dangerous light into the dark chamber of love. The hot oil scorches the beloved features, since we murder to dissect. And Psyche is for a punishment sent far below, to obtain from Persephone the secrets of happiness. But this casket turns out to contain something quite different: a dark secret, a sleep so potent no one can awaken from it. Now darkness is scattering through the universe, with the same velocity that a supernova scatters light.

13 Post-mortem

In the Crypt, the skeleton
from Flaxman's anatomical collection
sits legs apart in an iron chair
roaring with laughter
as shadows gather
round the Gothic archway of his skull.

Never thought he'd be so voluble
translated thus far from his living calendar.

But then
who am I to talk? [13]

---

[13] In the eighteenth century the mausoleum became a favoured motif. Country
houses built them as separate edifices, out on the greensward, in view of the main
windows. Often circular, with a peristyle of columns. Thus did the past embrace
the present. And thus did antiquity swallow modernity, if only in the forms con-
structed by the present for the disposal of its dead. Soane eagerly bought Seti's
tomb and installed it in the basement of his home. Then he threw his party. Can-
dles and chandeliers in their hundreds burned. The fashionable minds of London
marvelled at what Soane had here created: inside his Enlightenment home he had
assembled every item that might still appear to contradict the Age of Reason, in
any ultimate reckoning. Here in the sepulchral murk, Lord Thanatos was being
given his due. Burial grounds are the foundation stones of our civilization, and the
four corbel stones on the loggia outside spanned centuries in a matter of inches.
The ancient craft of masonry insists that there is always only a stone's throw be-
tween the living and the dead. Even our geometric reason acknowledges that those
triangles forming the pyramids remain the strongest of all known forms.

Yvonne Reddick

What Hughes Believed

That rowan is used to draw information from reluctant demons.

The wryneck is an ancient erotic charm.

The raven's cry means, "The farther I am from man, the better I feel".

Cultivating land drives out fairies.

To be humanised means to be denaturalised.

Foxes possess people in Japan by creeping in under their fingernails.

A fox once took the shape of a train on the Tokyo-Yokohama line.

Werewolves who stalk the University Library are called 'lupino-maniacs.'

A dream about a tiger coming down the hill, and knocking over your hut, will make you write about a jaguar.

In Scotland, Gruagach sprite-maidens often keep their souls in external things: three trout in a stream, or any bird on Ben Buidhe.

The tribes of Mount Elgon do not dream. Only their witch-doctor dreams, but he hasn't dreamed since the British came.

The Papuans think crocodiles have gone over to the British Government.

Apples symbolise Avalon, and poets' immortality.

That even in the midst of fierce flames the golden lotus may be planted.

Horizon

If any word could be found engraved around my skull, just above the ears and eyebrows, it would probably it would be the word 'horizon'.
    –Ted Hughes, 'The Rock'

My eyes have ached over your word 'horizon' all day.

'Horizon' flails its limbs
around an entomologist's pin
as it battles to squirm free,

it thrashes its syllables
casting black penumbras.

My office striplight strobes its glare.
The word curls around the 'i' in its midriff
where I have driven the pin.

Its fur heaves, the scroll of its tongue
protrudes. Small scales of powder
stipple the print on your page.

I will dissect it, needle out
the quick of its spirit. I must have work
to publish in *Critical Quarterly*, even if
I leave its wings maimed.

I feel your hand on my right arm,
heavy as a bolt of oakwood:
"Stop. You are destroying it."

Simon Perchik

*

Before each landing these stone steps
soften for mops and brushes
the way all feathers are preened

by heights and distances –this old tenement
is heated for 6 moons, 12 stars,1 stairwell
for each ascent, spreading it out

and though there is no fire
you dead still arrive as smoke
that now is the other way around

has become a river, on course
waiting for the wind to let go
touch down, suddenly dry your hands.

*

> "...to undress
> the river and
> place the water beside your body."
> Bruno K. Oijer

You cover your eyes the way this casket
reaches around from behind then falls
where the darkened water comes undone

as moonlight, spreads its make-believe
already filled with streams bitten into
by the small mouths guessing who

is standing beside what has become a lake
calling to the boat below that's not moving
though you are drowning in this bathroom mirror

that's waving its arms where there are no waves
from shipwrecks or oars or in your heart
some rope that's lost the sound from bells

could no longer pick up the bottom, tie it
to your bones that come only at night and knock
as the thud that cannot dry in the open.

*

You died with your eyes open
though the scream smells from salt
hidden in the chimes pulled by boats

and reefs that become waterproof
once they leave land the way shorebirds
track a fishing fleet and what's left

–these gravestones no longer move
are shining where a sea should be
could show the sun on your face

at low tide, waiting for you to let it rise
and from the wet dirt between your lips
finish the drink, swallow you whole.

*

Each night now, you arrive at the morgue
with pen an ink for the sheet stretched out
still wanting to tell how it happened

waits for you to pull up the same chair
the way each sentence will seal its words in place
as the silence that never had a chance

was burnt alive in the same straight line
arrows use to guide thirsty lovers
into each others arms with thunder

though it's your fingers now, still wet
rubbed down to the bone, bubbling over the name
coming back to life beside you.

*

You hold your shadow back, kept in
till the sun comes closer, stuffed
with light it can no longer carry

—it's then you let it go, empty your eyes
the way each evening in sorrow
makes room for those tears

not shallow enough to dry your heart
with salt, certain it will leach into the ground
as a river already dark, whose shadow

is pushing the Earth away, alone
an in a small wooden boat, tooth and claw
all these gravestones rowing it ashore.

Makyla Curtis

Dialoguing Deserts

a)
600 kilometres of apple trees and the cities dissolve. This sparse constellation is a suspension of southern winds, a barrier against sparse but icy sand, a mainly tussock strewn space on the road, no road, a never-ending road, heaping itself over hillocks.

b)
A hard-shouldered morning, with no road, a series of scarcities, literally, figuratively, figuratively, figuratively natural, nature-beamed and west. Just a constellation on a map.

c)
Like a chill effect of the poetry of known places, spaces. This is no frost, only a tussock, haumata, an intersection of darkness beneath a perplexed moon.

d)
To the drying poem, salted and hung up: a city's winter voice receives the Whangaehu that gurgles and roars indefinitely.

(Haumata is a variety of tussock grass. Whangaehu is a river that runs through the central North Island of New Zealand.)

ten

(i)
I disappear into the wash
of an imbued summoning
to rain is no end in terms of a poem

binaries regurgitate transparency
their denomination is a bank

(ii)
a similarity
on a separating moon
the longer visual forms a rise

(iii)
but wants
a language often: a language often
to buy outside, to buy today
now a language
deeply
transparent
that leaves in eaves are loved
and prayer concentrates with

(iv)
motor-hands like a fat resonance
in a river fishing up binaries
to make aquifers like there will be
some other change

encoding is smoking
a foaming sea, and I later disappear

(v)
from this height I bow
into a separating wisp

later there is rhetoric in gravel
that is dumped, to be spread
but pools
and cannot be moved

the gravel mist and moment,
leavening bread to multiply
new deals in language

(vi)
significance can be driven from supper:
attempts at such interpretations
fill the lung up with
pink salmon to
open another neurologist but

(vii)
the elements of the sea-like poem
are perhaps where such a low guessed simile
would be better truly violet

speaking where, there, along shells
with rescue written in white
a privilege baked in

(viii)
I am making cry
something to cry
I am making the ravens multiply like
tree limbs, branching a rhetoric
like the tide

(ix)
the warmth remains feeling
forgotten
climbing between wisps of sunset and
patient alibis
turning the tidal plum
between word meals
and speaking bridges

(x)
the low beam is guessed at
with smoked originality tied up
in the ceiling for preservation
it will taste of warm
but forgettable
stimuli.

Alasdair Paterson

My Life in Russian

That was when I lived near the big river. Don't ask why or how, it was just because.

That river was old school – a meander towards its annual ice quota, grumbling away underneath. We'd walk out on the thick ice and cut a hole. Fish, in a paroxysm of boredom, would open their mouths to the hook. We took our crepuscular trophy pictures. Life of man. Life of fish. Half-life of isotope.

There was nothing shoddy about that ice, though. It endured. Where it made its last stand, in the heart of the river, they would set charges to crack and rumble downstream. Think of the arc *basso profundo* makes from Last Judgement to your gut. Or ice-breaker waves of vodka shaking the tongue loose. Or the munitions of Spring.

The Spring of the air. The Spring of the birds. The Spring of the riverboat wakes, fanning out like flourishes from a swaggering accordion played by a friend who's not quite sober, to lap the feet of birches skittish in their dance-hall queue. The Spring of the captain, emerging from his winter hibernation among the furs and pickled mushrooms. He walked the gangplank all smiles – gold gold gold gold.

In the passenger saloon, a land of spirits and murky views, down where words burned recklessly, some rhapsodised about the river – all we can learn from it, how it waits patiently, steadfastly, to slip its ice-shackles and wrap itself in green. Others would say – the real lesson, surely, is the persistence of ice.

And me, the minority party of one, back on the promenade, who thought both schools of thought could be right, but then, what of it? And skimmed a stone towards the meltwater and celebrated its unlikely teeter for that moment and that moment and just that moment more. Ripples. Chords. And not forever.

My life as a former person

Welcome to the bar of former people. You'll find us here most nights. It's a home from home, for the likes of us. More homely, if anything. No knock at the door. And if I say, I was someone once – well, weren't we all, in here? It's congenial, in a manner of speaking, to a way of thinking.

Here's all about the manner of, the way of. We speak and think, therefore. That world outside, the cold, vexing place we say is just not what it was, and all about the way it was, yes, when we were someone, that's everything we have to talk about. Lucky that the topic's inexhaustible. We never lose the thread. We could go on and on. We do. Stories we've told before, ten times, a hundred times, they make the building blocks of evenings we've lived before, ten times, a hundred times, and they grow too, these stories, stretching out like the best to keep us on our toes, to pick up more and more of the shoogly detritus from the back of our minds, fragments pulled in by the magnetic force of the need to recollect, to reconstruct each someone who's been someone.

We might as well be drinking embalming fluid, we may in fact be drinking embalming fluid, there's no sell-by date for that here. We could be interested in today's deal on bitters. There's usually one. We've seen it all and it wasn't so bad, once. No rush to drink up and be gone. Not while we can still taste that world outside a little, between sips. Wormwood. Ashes. Gun metal. We'll build the stories up between us, building to The Story, the composite that gets it 360 degrees. Our lives and times. The story that each of us secretly longs to see and still hopes will never be complete. Because then, what?

Pull up a chair. There's always someone who won't be back. From out there. It's not safe, you know. Now, we assume you must be here for a reason. Should we know you from somewhere? From before? Are you one of the blamed, the forsaken, the forgotten? Are you in fact a bona fide former person? You were someone once, you say. We know, we know. Weren't we all, in here?

Annabel Banks

On Hebrews 13

Any god that keeps you going is a good god by me, except when choices rattle like dice in a chalice. Throw a three, say a prayer, throw again. Take those pictures down from the wall, the banners from the hall. Is it true that you're a finger-pie brain tweaker, reluctant jovial ready-speaker, cloying programme cult leader? Thirteen step breeder? Any god that keep you bowing is a good god, so have you taken on that role? Does your disapproval keep them from falling down that hole of misery and death? Do your words mark flesh? I know a son who knocked another to the ground so he wouldn't be late for your laying on of handy hot drinks—shocking, yes, but I have experience of promised pressure to tick my lists, so perhaps could understand your brand of love, even though I velvet-glove my cold ferrous fists. But then I don't metabolise, metastasise like you. We're systematically different, despite our origin-myth sympathies, that same cracked cradle. It's fucking fascinating, truth be told. I wonder how your day has gone today.

Mind Reading

This happens all the time. A red dress, fitted correctly. Perhaps my first tour through your dusty house moves a mouth well prepared with farewells. Don't bring bread into it, or arguments about the philosophy of art, but invite some tenderness to get bitten on the back, much too hard, while we lead our ignorant armies up to bed.

This has happened again. When I can laugh at your structured ladders, boxes, but nothing after that, it's like some madman's decision to miss the train. Enough to recall a hand on the cheek, loudly ignored armpits, the invitation to preen. My height, adjusted to reflect magnificence, became a confirmed ending, and I would remind you of my eyes but can't see you any more.

This is happening now. We watch the speeches. Flout the stink-mouth rule by eating my wrist. There is always more art, more science. We make darkness in the dark.

"Some Good Stuff Here"

For RML

Writing a poem for you means I'll breathe out like you,
unlunging a process beyond myself. Glue mischief down
with sneaky cut-up phrases imported, unboxed, then write
by smashing that green glass ball no one wanted, the one

left on the highest shelf. Dustpan and brush is a collocation
I can't clean up. Am I allowed to say I tried? It's a pain, though.
Later, in the pub, Carter suggests that pauses are immoral. I agree,
but not immediately. The students are practising necromancy again

and though I'd love this last stanza to get really fluffy, open out
with inclusive statements, (love as a leaf, shared human frailties,
fucking is dangerous, and so on,) I'll resist. It's SO hard. That snail
has been on the bathroom wall all week. I'll heat up my coffee now.

Norman Jope

Addis Ababa

I am there and not there, walking pocked pavements with the weary and the wary, listening to Mulatu Astatqe's ethno-jazz and thinking back to the florid shirts of the early Seventies. I have no sense of the geography of this city that I wander in, stared at by sad-faced young men in brown jackets and disdained by Abyssinian maids with brightly-coloured headscarves. I have no clear sense of a centre, and Le Corbusier boulevards give way to shacks and corrugated panels. Signs declaim wares in syncopated English, and the eyes of jackals are upon me as I parch – or so I imagine. Not one of the seven million inhabitants can lead me out of this labyrinth. I reach into my pocket and all that it contains is sand from the Danakil Desert.

Cherkos, Kebena, Urael, Kazanchis… I drift from district to district, dodging vendors whose goods I cannot afford to buy this evening. So can I bluff my way into the Sheraton, 'the best of the best' and revive myself in a marble bath? Or beg and cajole my way to a plate of fasting *wat*? Night will fall soon. I wander up Churchill Avenue, with its most English of names post-liberation, asking myself if it was ever Via Mussolini.

I colonise this city with my dérive, like an Emperor who, with a sweep of his hand, claims lands the size of Spain from his raft. The city will be named after me when I am dead (I hallucinate) and the Lion of Judah will roar at my graveside.

To be there and not there at all, wanting to be there in the land of antelopes, strolling like a ghost as rain begins to fall.

Mombasa

The first thing one notices are wires, strung across the outside of buildings like spaghetti.

Then shutters, balconies, a man in a basketball shirt pushing a trailer down a street. A child in an orange top, waving at no-one in particular.

Walking through the Old Town, I notice more spectacular balconies. Tattooed with intricate carvings, they are set in dove-white walls. Sweat pours into my eyes. My throat is a chasm of dryness through which I plunge.

Dazed, I pass charcoal sellers and tuk-tuks, my mind besieged by Coca-Cola signs and urgent graffiti. The city is strung together with wires. It fizzes and sparkles with its connectivity.

In the market, black-clad female vendors shelter under enormous parasols. I look up at closed shutters and hallucinate myself inside their shaded rooms, as old as I have ever been and as young as in the days of the Morris Minor.

Shop-signs are painted on white walls – the roughly-drawn barber shears his customer. The weight in my head is thickening. My hair is matted with sweat from my indolent brow.

Inside Fort Jesus, I rest amongst cannons and palms, anonymous behind its ochre walls. Outside, the sea conducts its trade with the wind.

Invisible wires go through my skull and it is as though I will never leave. The messages of this frenetic, faded port will remain mysterious, coming clear only in whispers.

Old Stones, White Roads
Kraków, March 2013

On the train from the airport, snow dribbled down the window and the suburbs, as if engrossed in chaos, welcomed me with a yawn of ice and graffiti. The station was depopulated, as if constructed for my entrance alone.

Then I sat at the window of a suburban hotel, wondering why it was that, at the end of March, I had been unlucky enough to encounter this whiteness. I had convinced myself, when booking the flight, that I would relax under a café umbrella in early spring sunshine.

Instead, the blue tram approaches the centre and I disembark, head bowed against sleet with the Wawel to my left. And I traipse the Royal Route – almost deserted in the late afternoon of Easter Sunday – wiping slush from my glasses, trying to find words for the discoloured ochre shades of the buildings.

The city, at least, is hushed and serious. In the Rynek, sleet intensifies before turning to a freezing, flatulent rain that blurs my vision. Old stones, white roads, a handful of tourists under bright umbrellas inspecting stalls… I circle the edge before turning back in search of somewhere warm, cheap and authentically Polish in which to eat.

The city's make-up has been washed away. Its reality is all that I am left with – buildings that seem as immutable, today, as the stones of a tor. I can almost pretend that I am not a tourist, but a secular pilgrim to a place of epiphany.

Kazimerz

Set apart from the rest of the city, this neighbourhood is one in which ghosts have left footprints. The former occupants are gone, whether driven out or murdered – but it is recovering meaning, acquiring a modified identity as a place in which a Jewish renaissance meets the bohemian Poland of the twenty-first century.

We dine on borscht and potato pancakes in the Arial restaurant, to a murmur of klezmer muzak. The whip-cracking masters have been warded off for good and, as they shrink into the chronicles, their forms acquire the ephemerality of cobwebs. *They lost*, I eulogise – their totalising madness a distant memory, our casual presence here a riposte to their megalomania.

But, for anyone who knows a little of the history of this place, the death it contains is indelible. And how can we ever know where our own death resides? Can any place, however redeemed, escape that undertow?

I think of Trakl – found dead from an overdose in a military hospital in this city, in 1914, he was buried for a decade in the Rakowicki Cemetery – a tram ride to the north – before being re-interred near Innsbruck. If he had been told in 1913 that Kraków, the Galician capital and leading city of *Modra Polska*, would be the place in which he would meet his end – how surprised would he have been?

I, too, could die here in an instant – here one moment, falling to the ground the next – and there would be worse places, and even worse nights, I morbidly conclude although the time is always too soon. And tonight, at least, I escape – if not from the outnumbering dead.

Susan Connolly

```
m   m  t           p        cl
mm mm  h          p e a         o
mmmmm  e         p e a c o         u
mmmmm          p e a c o c k       d
mmm m  m        s c r e e c h
mmm m  a        s c r e e
mmmmm  i         s c r                      s
mmmmm  d           s                     s u n
m mmm  e                                   n
m mmm  n                                        s
mmmmm                                        s e t
mmmmm  t                                       t
m mm   o
m mm   w   the   the   the   the   the   the   the   the   the   the
m mm   e   CrookCrookCrookCrookCrookCrookCrookCrookCrookCrook
mmmmm  r   road road road road road road road road road road
         caravan      caravan                        t        b
         c  av  n     c  av  n                     a         o
         carav  n     carav  n                   o         a
         O    O    O    O                      b         t
                                             b o a t
r i v e r      r i v e r      r i v e r      r i v e r      r i v e r
 i v e r        i v e r        i v e r        i v e r        i v e r
  v e r          v e r          v e r          v e r          v e r
   e r            e r            e r            e r            e r
    r              r              r              r              r

    b        r            r            r            r
  eee      r i          r i          r i          r i        w
  aaaaa    r i v        r i v        r i v        r i v       o
  ccccc    r i v e      r i v e      r i v e      r i v e     m
  ooooo    r i v e r    r i v e r    r i v e r    r i v e r   a
  nnnnn                                                       n
wallwallwallwallwallwallwallwallwallwallwallwallwallwallwallwallwallwall
allwallwallwallwallwallwallwallwallwallwallwallwallwallwallwallwallwall
llwallwallwallwallwallwallwwllwallwallwallwallwallwallwallwallwallwallwa
lwallwallwallwallwallwallwallwallwallwallaallaallaallwallwallwallwallaallaalla
```

42

the seawall, Baltray

standing on the seawall at Baltray,
looking at Mornington,
the Maiden Tower and the caravans,
fishing boats upside down
on mussel shells

```
                                                      mm
                                                     moon
                                                    moooon
                                                    moooon
                                                     moon
                                                      nn
        s              s
        h              h
        i              i
   shipshipshipshipship
    shipshipshipshipsh
     shipshipshipship
      shipshipshipsh
```


```
 w        s                  w        s                    moon
    a        e                  a        e                  moooon
 s        v        a        s        v        a         moooon
    e        e                  e        e                  moon
       a        s                  a        s               nn


 w        s                         b        w        s
    a        e                     eee          a        e
 s        v        a              aaaaa      s        v        a
    e        e                    ccccc          e        e
       a        s                 ooooo             a        s
                                  nnnnn

 w        s              llwa  r                  v     e    wall
    a        e           wall     i                  e      llwa
 s        v        a     llwa  i  v                     r   wall
    e        e           wall     v  e                      llwa
       a        s        llwa  v  e     r                   wall
       a                 wall     e  r                      llwa
 s  a  d                 llwa  e     r                  r   wall
       n        a        wall     r                  r      llwa
          s  a  n  d     llwa  r                  r  i      wall
                n        wall               r  i           llwa
 nesting  terns          llwa           r  i     v         wall
 sting  terns  ne        wall              i     v         llwa
 ing  terns  nest        llwa  r                  v  e     wall
 g  terns  nestin        wall     i                  e     llwa
 terns  nesting          llwa  i  v                     r  wall
```

44

towards the sea

walking the wall towards the sea,
on my left the noisy nesting terns –
and far off, a container ship,
waiting for the high tide

Joey Connolly

Starry

A lyric which is at best a silk
settled over and then staplegunned into
    the flaking MDF poster-board of tradition.

Tradition at best a five-cent gumball machine
stocking only the acetic taste of anxiety. All round an antiquity,
    which is bestwise a history-staid quintessence

of luxury. Luxury which barely conceals these
thriving bibelots of worry,
which at best are only a tawdry excitement which at best
  is only a kitschy exemplar of the rush to lay a hand

or leastwise finger on the special cornucopia
  of the plastic and the various
    and the well-intentioned: the tenured chemist

smiling through his test-tubes   the
  sweet-sharp scent of alkanes   and esters
  drifting from his faculty-funded fume cupboard,
    like smoke   from the corners of a film star   her
     collagen lips   her signature brand

her   gracious acceptance of a bouquet of asters,
her gracious acceptance a bouquet of asters,
  it is the same complaints again.

  We know nothing but it is synthesised.
Which is never a critique, only a curtseyed portrait
of the singing child, her dear dangling teddy-bear.

Order

The vaguely schizoid dualism which seems essential
for understanding any text which fails to engage
this nervous clay we're of. The spiralling of seashells
and galaxies alike are lost upon the vitamin H

or flavordynamic which spun them into being. It's cruel –
the small determined girl forbidden from pressing
the buttons of lifts – that the universe has all these rules
precluding the felted hammers for our heartstrings

from the nimble fingers of the cytosines
which built them. Except this: we are machines

constructed so that matter may know itself. Adore
the nerves, but adore as well the clay the nerves lay bare.
Oh future little one, okay!, let's stop at every floor
and explore the crazy décor there.

Adam Day

Dead Friesian in Winter

Far from the cusp of the tractor
path, beside an empty creek, propped
against a pin-oak like a fireplace aslant

to the chimney of a toppled house.
Still steaming, the nose firm
glistening, the hips going. Gray

tongue thick, purple
in morning darkness, where needles of light
strike the bulk of the wrenched

head, reaching its knees to disappear
in a moving mist. The grass
a frozen crust, corn arched

and angled into a field's naked
girders and beams, a stone wall
in wet snow where blackbirds argue.

Braunvieh

She turns in the doorway
buttoning her blouse,
a mouth-sized bruise
at her breast. Outside
a cow has dropped green dung
wet over a bucket of cherries
left by the spigot – in the rain
it smokes a little. The sun
is perched on a crest

of thunderheads. She's walked
now into the harsh light
of the kitchen's bare bulb
and I am sitting like a scarecrow,
like a man shot through
the cheek, naked-legged.
Not ten minutes earlier
a bull jumped that cow
and their throttling
sent them thudding against
the clapboards, clattering
over the cellar door, a hoof
put clean through to the fetlock –
a wind brought the smell
of them in–the bull's slobbery
head, the clumsy hot
lowing throat gulps.

When Kids

We'd shoot rock pigeons off the house
gutters, as they crouched, considerate

or squat to shit and they'd fall through
the spidering branches, a kind of twin of itself

like looking at another man's penis at the urinals,
or at his girlfriend. But it's ok because he doesn't

notice, and she has a tag of dark hair
at the small of her back, and that's ok

because she's got nice tits. Back then
in Milwaukee, one of Dahmer's boys escaped

naked, bloody, and when he caught up
to the boy, the cops had arrived

but sent the couple on their way for
just another lover's quarrel. An elderly

neighbour, hard of hearing, described the almost
owl-like human cries. The stars slumped,

the trains dumb. Somewhere near, a porch light
and the raccoon beneath it. Eating signals appreciation –

we smoke and eat the pigeons – the powerful
chest muscles make good meat – nothing goes

to waste. And we know what the girlfriend does
with her man and what he does, too.

David Rushmer

The Memory in Our Wings

        as if the possibility
were birthing its own ghost

the ether
        to give up
        all material bodies

        human documents,
                beams of spinal light
                        relinquish them
                        against the corpuscular theory

                it goes, without saying.

        in the form of waves
                & the brutal loss
to injury.

We carry the memory in our wings.

II

wound, spread,
    where
    the tongue formed
the branching vessels of language
  attached to the mother,

son followed
earth.

the paper bodies

  bloody containers of matter
    open, burning

    night recovered
      his voice
in lightning veins
asunder.

We carry the memory in our wings.

The Drift

        drift into thinking
     at intervals only

Souvenirs translated as nightmares

           when he speaks
       of what he has not yet discovered

       verbal coincidence
          or vapour

       being diffused into the body,
       between the outer and the inner world

View of the sun: the same obscurity.

Palimpsest

opening,
              this haunted body
method of the book

    spore blooming, tongue blossomed
words source   their surface
                              as the skin is scraped

        archaeological.

    spaces and depths
              in language
                    she finds

                    reading a composition
        on the skull

        structure is
              material

                        the silences
                    engraved

Peter Riley

On Islands

(i) Bardsey

You walk above in the light
on soft ground, creatures of thought
glowing off the sea and the distance
to be gained. Haze on the fields
spreading upwards.

What we do here: live, more days,
climbing the stairs to the bed-loft each night
and lying there, waiting for
events in the sky. On the morning window-ledge
sunlight falls through a seagull's wing.

Days and nights of wind and bird sound
the sea pushing its lines towards the land
a hundred and twenty-one seals in the bay.
And out of all this a speaking to a purpose
out of this a reciprocal song.

Saints buried under the track, streaks
of limestone in the grass. Who went
unrecorded, whose being lives
somewhere else, far away, Doncaster
or Freetown, in acts of heartedness.

Strange birds fill the night with cackling
and squeaking over our thin roof. We lie
in the loft trying not to sleep until the sky

is quiet again, dream components
drifting towards the island.

The birds are Manx shearwater and they
know their tunes by heart all over the night.
The form of thought that they represent
mentions global fidelity and the price
of groceries at this time of year.

Massed voices from the sea, statements about the world
in scribbled notes blown out of the hand, lost in the wind
found again in a book or a bone flute. Decked
in red and white bands the unmanned lighthouse
attracts migrating birds to their death at night.

To stay and get older, learning the details, of sea currents,
cloud formations, whereabouts of the hut circles on the hill.
And to sit on the bench against the harbour shed
in late sunshine watching the lobster boat coming in,
without candy floss, without writers in residence.

To stay and get older day by day as the
mind quickens to the task and acts
of judgement become acts of justice.
How does this happen? By what principle
as delicately toned as a blackbird's egg.

Salt corroded iron ring in a stone stump,
bright red. Cist burials in the shoreline bank.
Catch my breath before it blows away. Trust
the principle. Leave the door unlocked all night.
Only the sea breeze will visit. Be sure to vote.

Alert at night in the loft, free of the eyes' commands
breathing like sleeping babies, thoughts always open,
always clear, thoughts you bring with you,
language that pursues you and here
come those crazy birds again.

We lie here and things happen
elsewhere, nothing can stop them.
Guilt dated 1945 and more massacres.
A voice is nothing unless appointed.
Sea murmuring and hissing grass,

There is no voice. There is no sense of.
The sea's eyes are closed under the soles
of your thought, year after year inching the self
towards a question to be asked about what is shared.
Wind. Birdsong. Death Stones.

That's no answer. There is no answer.
There is no silence. Listen to the mad
cacophony of the shearwater, making
species calls to their young all night,
island night, is it you are you there?

When day comes, listen. Listen
to the grass. Listen to the gravestones.
There is a whispering about the isle
that delights and harms not,
clearest at night, when the mind takes its part

And clear in the day when it rains.
Look it up in a dictionary, write
to the newspapers, tell us the facts,

getting older, moving slowly,
all comfort beyond.

This word and that and some others
and I sense an approaching proposition
creeping here under cover of night,
but everything I think is interrupted
by two thousand rubber ducks in the sky.

Creatures of thought, raging in the night sky
stamping your syllables into the soil
from which emerge baby birds and fly away
over thousands of miles of ocean bearing thoughts
that all may yet be the best it can.

Lucy Hamilton

from The Diarists

Crocodiles & Frigate Birds

It's years since the Diarist last saw it. Men had to manoeuvre it *[one good tree & axe for hollowing]* through trap-doors up to the third floor, winch it up on ceiling-rollers in two, or was it three, pieces? It's the only object of his on display in the museum *[long planks from single tree]*, one small notice with his name and the year of the Expedition. No items of clothing *[pieces of rattan]*, no diaries or sophisticated instruments. When they were small her awestruck children fingered the intricate crocodile *[carved beast for figurehead]* and the frigate birds in perpetual flight. Now the canoe is suspended so high you can't see inside *[wooden weights, hooks, scrapers, thwarts, brackets]*. Last night they all crowded round, skyping a granddaughter in Bolivia. And she could see her face and hear her voice. It's amazing what that little 'periscope' can do.

Notes & Quotes

The Diarist's son owns a fibreglass sports kayak. When he goes. When he goes white-water kayaking in the Atlas Mountains. Only a Greenlandic kayak is called *qajaq*. C's kayak would be *qajariaq* meaning 'like a *qajaq*'. Each man's qajaq is built to the specifications of his own body. *I always tried to make it so that it was not too short – so that I could load the insides with skins and provisions.* The Inuit copy the animals – that ivory bear Uncle Tom sent for her 10th birthday! – match the skins to parts of their own body. The women stitch a seal-gut jacket – *tuilik* – with bone-needle. Sew two-layered leather stitching not to hole the fabric. To retain water-tightness. To stiffen where necessary. C. wears his neoprene wetsuit & jacket. When he goes whitewater kayaking on the Oued

Ouzoud. When he wears his fibre-glass crash-helmet. When he plunges between rockfaces. Flies between water & sky.

Bedtime Stories

I

And the Diarist smiles, seeing as vividly as yesterday their eager little faces pleading to hear again & again: *In the worst and deepest of the rapids, we touched a sunken tree, upset, and the canoe went careering bottom up down the stream.* The father she hardly knew ... *I got caught in some of the underwater branches of the tree, was dragged deep down to where it was horrible and quite dark* ... How still they lay and rapt, eyes wide as owls'. Oh, the times he escaped by a feather! *I was carried along by the current at a hideous pace towards another swift and deep rapid ... which would certainly have been the end of me, had the Dyak not caught sight...*

II

Not a day goes by that she doesn't think of Mother. Mother who was 'waiting until you were old enough to understand'. Standing at the fireplace, turning her face away to tell what N. already knew – but he hadn't believed the boy at school. Now it was true. He would never forgive. Not until he'd eventually write the book ... *Ironically Dr. S. became better known for his appalling death than for his distinguished life.* Mother descending the stairs crying ... *For us she published a selection of his letters & diaries.* Now it's the grandchildren reading *The canoe was recovered, but the sack containing my bedding and everything else was lost.*

Sabiyha Rasheed

Dutchman Jumbee

Dutchman Jumbee dug fingernails in soil and taste the hot earth. Dutchman Jumbee take *land of many waters* and drink until he sick. Dutchman Jumbee heave into Essequibo, the water blister and cry. Dutchman Jumbee take blue of Essequibo to push into his eye. Amerindian wash with Essequibo water and their skin become Dutchman skin. Amerindian contours mapped on trees and Dutchman say he grow it. Dutchman tree with Dutchman lung, steal Guyana air. Dutchman breath woven into silk of Guyana's heat and light. Dutchman want Amerindian hair to tie wrist and neck. Amerindian fade into Guyana soil, become paths under Dutchman feet.

Dutchman Jumbee throw rope across sea and drag Africa by the neck. Dutchman howl shatter the moon to rain on purple night skin. Dutchman Jumbee hide in Dutchman tree when blackness become blacker. Black man sing with Guyana winds to make Dutchman skin shake. Dutchman chew on black man tongue so he never sing again.

Dutchman jumbee burning leaves
Making ash of all its beauty

Carving red, gold and green into forearms
Of those who got caught in the rope

Pickney Tongue

Pickney tongue, wet and sour
Sharper than cutrass blade
Drip and spit staccato shards
To cut the coolie nigger skin
And draw faces in the blood

Coolie water rice
To Pig Tail, Brown Girl
Nigger man sala
To Black Boy, Scabby Knee

Wash your beatie with dahl and rice
Pink lip on dark boy let out laugh
That fly and sting like marabunta

Teef your mommy ten dollar
Coolie gal play jump rope
Jumping on nigger boy ribs

Mango yellow, mango green
Plantain yellow, plantain green
Still mango, still plantain
Pickney coolie, pickney nigger
Still pickney
Bleeding
Red, gold and green

Moongazer

When Moongazer stood, with his hands resting on his narrow hips, he thought of nothing but night, and what accompanied it. Thin rolls of skin would appear at the back of his neck as he tilted his head upwards to inhale the dark. He stood taller than Guyana's largest tree, back muscles flexed and legs parted. His eyes filled with moon rocks and the heat of the stars that peppered the sky. He sometimes imagined the moon as a fruit that he wished to take a bite of and watch moist flesh and moon lit liquid pour over Guyana's soil. On the nights when the sky seemed hollow, Moongazer would listen to the Moon's stories, of how he once lit the path for escape, had to hide when white hands tried to steal him from the sky and gave hope to those who only got a rare glimpse of him. The Moon's stories would make Moongazer weep until the sun emerged. His deep howls would echo for miles, causing restless nights. Moongazer became infuriated by the Moon's stories and resented humans for their cruelty. He promised the Moon he would protect him. He swore that if he were to look down and see anyone passing through his legs, walking towards the Moon, he would crush them between his calves and give their souls to the stars.

Moongazer kept his promise,
crushing bone to white powder

Letting blood feed the night
As they did in the day

juli Jana

she boards the train at belleville

I see her sandals first
a broad strip above the toes
the red nails neatly spaced
jeans rolled up at ankle

ignoring me she takes out pen & paper
I keep on writing so does she
her head slightly tilted
shoulders hosting black bra straps

we pause at the next station
watch the panning billboards
each searching for stimulus
I catch her eye   challenge her quest

at anvers she gets off
a broad footed woman holding a fan
takes her place opposite   crosses her legs
uncrosses her legs   parts her knees
starts fanning up her dress
it is 37 degrees in paris

the circus barker

if you would oblige me a trifle
ladies & gentlemen
I would you listen to a story
I entreat you not to turn a deaf ear
there's a fish tale told by a fish
a toddler's rhyme recited by grandma
the weird & wonderful expounded by darwin

he'll even produce a monkey-man to prove it
or an elegy sung at a death bed
the girl with the goat has travelled far
to tell the story about man & beast
there is also the happy gathering for a chit-chat

the stars are out tonight

I would I had a voice to join the howling dogs
the costume of a fresh water fish
so I could offer you a dish from the swell
but if you get a-waking with your night legs
pausing at each stall each station
a character may be let out the bag
as old as an old sailor with a pipe
and a story as long as a line with a hook

there be an air of mystery
boys & girls the haunt of a melody
the stars are shining tonight

join the campfire
enthralled faces turned inward
pause at the camp bed to catch a strand of comfort
kneel in the lamp lit corner for ancient wisdom
sit on grandma's knee for the storybook tale
hover by the tents catching snippets
dance round the lighted circle

walk the dogs or the goats
there my be angels in the woods

the stars shine brighter tonight

heart of london

salisbury court fleet street
samuel pepys calls on a surgeon to remove a gall stone
he first uses a pipe up the penis to locate it
removes it with a pair of pliers – it gets used as a paperweight
1658

hole-in-the-wall tavern chandos street
claude du vall beloved highwayman of the ladies
having come from venice to charm with manners
is captured & hung – not even king charles II can save him
1670

jerusalem passage
coal merchant thomas britton stores coal a-plenty in his cellar
choral concerts held upstairs also a table for composing
coffee a penny a cup
1714

covent garden
boasts taverns theatres coffee shops 22 gambling dens 56 brothels
fair *rosamund sugarcunt* creates her own perfume
sells it to intoxicated love sick suitors
1722

bunhill gardens
dame mary page shows no fears at operations
is tapped 60 times yielding 240 gallons of water
she never complains & attains middle age
1728

green canister in half moon street
first sex shop sells flagellation machines & woman comforters in leather
also preservatives known as cundums
to stop the stream of bastard progeny especially for the royals
1732

gentleman's club white's in piccadilly
duke of queensberry courts ladies & wagers a wacky bet *short of time*
that within an hour a 4 wheeled carriage can cover 19 miles
he wins by using a whalebone & silk harness to lighten the load
1747

greek street 47
casanova arrives from venice setting up lodgings in london
advertises for young ladies claiming the art of seduction to be a
    profession
he belittles a troublemaker by parading a parrot shouting *charpillon*
    is a whore
1763

burlington arcade piccadilly
lord cavendish has the arcade erected for his wife to shop in safety
excludes rowdies who throw oysters & enforces a code of conduct
no whistling singing or opening of umbrellas
1819

upper floor execeter exchange   the strand
edward cross having a menagerie here in the city centre
has an ageing destructive elephant *chunee* dissected publicly
sells tickets for public to watch
1826

athenaeum club pall mall
honours the *duke of wellington* who defeated napoleon
by erecting a granite block to use in dismounting his horse
taking into account his old age
1830

royal aquarium & winter garden opposite westminster abbey
the entertainer *farini* uses a 14 year old girl *zazel* as a human
    cannonball
a distance of 30 feet by means of a long tube fitted with springs
crowds flock to see the spectacle
1877

audley square mayfair
at the height of the cold war the lamppost with a little trapdoor on
        the side
situated outside number 2 is used for message drops
by the russian secret service spies
1950-60

old kent road bermondsey
russell gray having been refused permission to build
installs a 35-ton T34 tank on a small plot
the council agreeing that he could have a tank on his property
1995

if thou art a male
look to thy purse
if thou art female
look to your
heart
        (casanova

Clark Allison

Experience, Again

I wanted to know
in order to do the right thing
in accord with the
perhaps inexplicable reality
if not mystery
of having been
brought into this life

experience may be many things
but it is not simply a game
and it is not lies
it is indeed
not what you say I am
experience, in short,
excceds and takes priority over
what they deem to regard
as social adjustment
or, you are not me
you perhaps haven't a clue
don't even know me
or, who do you think you are
claiming and lying
about these things
you don't own me

facticities feel the green sledge
mountain face curious among the dark
pilgrimage is it steep
am I getting it wrong again
letting (un)open or just tired
and pissed off
had enough of it
many props litter the stage

lots of seats but
are they empty
every time he looks
I feel like he wants something
maybe something I don't
and never will have
stay or go
when you can
we must make arrangements
maybe I should leave
for other pastures
or merely continue here
somewhere I can
lay my head
glacial rock run cool pool
amongst light against walls
puer/
cronus agon
multiplicities
countless variations
perhaps one can only
make of it what you will
or is it can
what's been
what's next

Linda Kemp

Archive of Separation I

instruction led to belief & apostrophe

Rarely basic data observes
her absence
contributing other forms
        or else
unusual applications seem to yield

ontogenetically proceeding from an end-
product, walk
        directly into phases of personality

s/he seems symptom & syndrome.

                Regularly in childhood
starting points entail
        radical end-stops,
present-day theory adjuncts
thought contributing to loss & trace
working prospectively.

Primary observations characteristic of the present
function as direct import

        it is important to know this

these psychical processes enter the consulting room
whilst adopting a neural stance separates twigs &
        drops off branches

s/he out theorises the theory

those trying offspring, spongy &
        how useful in proving 'yes
or no'
        thick description proves its own
properties
focusing on pathogens

bright
& a synthesis so strange
        the strange say impossible things
microphones
                doubt
& the doubling limitations of watching strength
in whose doubt accuracy races into traditional method.

Walk me home.

Archive of Separation II

Healthy
        & after systematic conditions the first
separates into either

                                studies occur in the ought
unlike possible observations the write-off
begins between age &
upsetting others,
a switchback to
uncertainty & other records,
afterward unsettling until describing in detail
little claws &
                soon after

in unfamiliar environments data collates
reasonable & secure
between two phases, describing the immediate &
the chancy

          acutely distressed, the rest
diminishes into concave laughter &
other lessons

                  quiet &
not because crumbling but neurobiologically
it's best

during subsequent visits the seat
languishes into lanes

untrammelled visitors leaf through gilt-bound
tomes & behaviour insincerely

each day he cried &
each day he appears the same

not much upset

in familiar environs the sheep are painful & yellow,
the eyes, eyes &
nothing left except, never
left in unfamiliar environs he looks about &
absence is evenings
familiar
& undoubted

insufficient levelling.

Archive of Separation III

Acceptance & her psychiatrist
conceptualise data
                            busy applying
possession
                    winking into making
excitation possesses

            character & mental functions
building concepts

so sure the sum
                        possess displacement
framing concepts switching diminution
tending to
switch into

the principle of inertia squats on the floor
relating closely held principles
into certainties
                        mental apparatus tends to

sucking &
increasing the primary governing body
who sits on the back step
sucking &
                        the process of discharge

quantitative & dreaming
perspective given

Archive of Separation IV

Since regard remains intact

        & itself unlike the physical

the cyclic model formulation

        fumigation as get-out clause

bankrupt & so disillusioned

        representing a primary principle

unable to roll out of bed

        the light-switch is a sure start

energy modelling utility

        & change. This model is an interpretation

of datasets

        & unfathomable statistical modelling

attempts an alternative.

        Whether it is supplementary or

theory of object-relations

        it is relational, a roll

explicitly theorising shortcomings

        & similarly employing

metaphors of graduation.

        Likewise

behaviour employs reflection

        signalling biological & theory.

Matthew Stoppard

Two Sonnets

Seeing *The Light* in The Star, York Road

There's filth and grace in
a pigeon feather
sent twirling by wind
where cousins gather
for a christening
in the ground-floor church,
a kickboxing gym
upstairs when you search
this art deco urn
containing ashes
of lovers, film fans;
pigeon flight becomes
ghost of a flicker –
movie projector?

Aerial stunt over The Regent

Burmantofts twilight
lingers like an ache
for those who catch sight
of the aeroplane
Attendance is high
on opening night,
six block letters lie
on the roof – don't fight
the urge to raise hands,
clutch falling paper;
our spectacle and
picturehouse never
could be seen for miles
now Al-Murad Tiles.

The Regent and The Star are two former cinemas in Leeds.

The Lyric without James

This idea is finding
a new ticklish bodypart
and now I'm here
more aware I miss
his half century of city
cabbies mistaking
him for a bouncer
doorman of our genre
O rhythmic hulk, you've
a grandmother that shares
an East Midlands elbow
with me, umbilically
linked to my birthplace
avoiding this moment
sunlight behind pink lettering
the shadow of LYRIC
across my forehead looking up.

* *The Lyric on Tong Road, Leeds, operated as a cinema for 66 years. Poet James Morgan Nash has operated as a human being for the same amount of time. The above poem is 66 words long.*

Liz Adams

Automatic Myth

After Ethel Schwabacher

Swollen with a *warm rain* the mind floods pink and a stroke
of grey. Pain draws you into myth, into darkness, into a light
you hunger for. Summon up a god and the colours relate
or the woman's face blooms; the floral nature of the design
becomes eyes and trembled cold reminding the viewer
of some chase through time where Eurydice fails to come to the sweeter
calls of Orpheus. Forget the stone of circles for this is dynamism:
how the stars vibrate whilst pain is always fertile purple crinkles
upwards on another canvas my right eye patrols like the shaking yellow
that announces arrival is all *Seasons and Days*; in the way that myth
moves back through symbol and the unconscious is always remembering,
like the stone moving towards liquidity there is some kind of dance
and the city dances always, but to tell you that automatically
these colours and how far they reach across the music halls of that day,
where the sky shakes with gold and purple-red explodes within all heart.

Green Stripe

After Barnett Newman and Patrick Jones

using a flashy red was what he wanted but to make
it unflashy and mix it with carmine stand in front with
a walrus and a dicky bow, find some forgiveness
inside the tribe, *the most amazing fuck up* is what
it leads to; against each nerve my breath moves –
there was never much gentleness in poetry, perhaps
that was one thing it didn't contain; beauty is different

each stem of the tulip moves and hushes, hushes and moves,
each delinquent lilac fogs the vase on the desk with the daisy
etched on with light, Cézanne with his shapes and *a man of light*:
the cubist model or vision; imagine the way a painter's mind
reacts to the sea or an estuary the 'oceanic feeling' that engulfs
a speck of an essence is the relief from the rigid holding
of the desk, the rigid judge that sits in the head with his wooden
hammer and list of convictions is a portrait of any *good* patriarch

I sleep in that kind of red, folded around the imagination
I become closer to my father, closer to the pretence of heaven
closer to the daisy fields of Patagonia where three juts
of granite sit upon a lake of changing Rothkos, then suddenly
it was all dark again with a green stripe pulling up the middle
not an emerald in sight just the stripe so green, so lovely, how
beautiful that stripe was, it held every building, every *because*
it made its way upwards and didn't look back, the ascent

held the nerves in every particle, the ascent was filled with origami
swans: their eyes full of possession, their hissing reaching out over
the slide of the estuary where the little egret made her way
stepping lightly over the velvety mud, the avocets pointing their
long beaks down towards every crustacean; a washed up shark,
so blank and its rage long gone; the view of Starcross or the stars
in their darkness pointing outwards, their vision not consigned
to any pretences of the everlasting, of any pretence of eternity

Kenny Knight

A Supermarket in Honicknowle

What thoughts I *had* of you tonight, Walt Whitman
    Allen Ginsberg, 'A Supermarket in California'

So where are you tonight
Allen Ginsberg
now that the supermarket has closed
and Santa Claus has gone back home
to wrap up warmly for Christmas
and the checkout girl from California
has flown across the Atlantic
to spend New Year in America
with the store detective
from your imagination.

Are you on the same flight
reading *Sunflower Sutra*
or out in the car park with Jack
waiting for a train
that passes through
the Nineteen Fifties
or are you pushing
shopping trolleys across the night
to distant high streets of the heart.

Are you working in a supermarket
or selling sunflowers
at the end of a switchboard line
chanting Buddhist mantras
over the tannoy
to get yourself through
another supermarket day
your voice moving
from department to department

calling workers on the shop floor,
workers in short-sleeved shirts
dressing shelves
and serving images to customers
or are you working the night shift
trying to make ends meet
like two old friends on a street corner.

So where are you tonight
Allen Ginsberg
are you haunting the dreams
of the next generation of writers
reading poetry
in dream supermarkets of the night
as you cruise the aisles
shopping for inspiration
filling your shopping trolley
with sunflower oil
and Valentine cards
for everyone you've ever loved.

And where are they now
where are all of my old
teenage friends from childhood
those cowboys from the corner shop.
I've not seen any of them for generations.
Are they happily married to television
or out walking the streets,
homeless shadows looking for shelter
and strangers to love.
Have they been consumed
by the Consumer Society
recycling themselves like Himalayan monks
or egg boxes in the cardboard bailer.
Have they fallen
into the black hole of capitalism
like Harpers garage
and Pete Russell's Hot Record Store.

I'm working in a supermarket now
serving lunch to Mrs. Flatfish,
The Witch and the Wardrobe
and the Five to Five Man
working with my grand-daughter
reading *Guthrie to Ginsberg*
and other poems in church halls
and libraries
all the way from the Honicknowle Hills
to the outskirts of town,
but I've never read
in a Supermarket in California
or in the dining room of the Beat Hotel.

I remember the night you shared the stage
with Peter Orlovsky at the Lower Guildhall
on the corner of Catherine Street
and I remember that night
wanting to hear the lonesome whistle
of a locomotive replace the car horns
and scooters on Royal Parade
remember wanting to hear you read
Howl and *Sunflower Sutra*
for the Buddhists and the beatniks,
the prehistoric penguins
and the train spotters
wearing halos of nostalgia
and long hair in the crowd,
but you didn't read
any of that old City Lights stuff
or bring Gregory Corso,
Lawrence Ferlinghetti
or the store detective from California
out from behind the curtains
to make their debuts
at the Lower Guildhall,
no trio of Penguin Modern Poets
no bunches of sunflowers

no shoplifters in the crowd
crossing the car park
with books of poetry.

That night at the Lower Guildhall
as we passed through evening stardust
you drew a sunflower
two or three inches tall
a black sunflower from America
which took root like a memory
and found a home
on the windowsill of my room
overlooking the park
and one afternoon
as March gave way to April
I found a packet of sunflower seeds
in a corner of old shadows
in my father's garden shed
which I planted
to brighten the neighbourhood
a galaxy of sunflowers
constellations of them
all over the slopes
of Honicknowle and West Park.

The sunflower you drew is thirty years old now
thirty years since I stood in front of the stage
with Allen Clarke and Bernard Brotherton
and smoked cigarettes with Peter Orlovsky
until he realised it wasn't weed.

Tim Allen was there
unknown to me then
one of two hundred strangers
in the beat poetry crowd,
but I didn't see the store detective
was he hiding backstage
or lingering by the bookstall

did he follow you
periodically through the years
until his shadow grew thin.

Before I read you I knew nothing
about supermarkets or sunflowers
knew nothing about Lorca,
Whitman or Kerouac.
By the time I'd negotiated
the foothills of adolescence
I'd read snatches of T.S. Eliot,
Alfred Noyes and Ogden Nash
and listened to the blues singer
Bessie Smith
in Kenny Frost's house
on Shakespeare Road
when I was fifteen and still at school
and now I'm approaching sixty
and my shadow is pointed
towards the supermarket
and the moon is following me
across the still forms
of sleeping policemen in the road

and you where are you tonight
Allen Ginsberg
are you walking home
with all those other beat poets of the night
while I'm walking around in crazy circles
outside a supermarket in Honicknowle
under the constellation of the sunflower
from where Walt Whitman sends his regards.

The Old Wooden Bridge

In summer I fish for nothing
off the edge of the old wooden bridge
the past sits to the right
the future on the left
three pairs of feet dangling into space.

Bobbie Gentry's *Ode to Billie Joe*
I sing to myself and the river adds
a bit of Handel to the mix.

On the old wooden bridge
on the bus into town
I read stories by Khalil Gibran
and Mullah Nasrudin.
Elsewhere I read
Lewis Carroll to the rabbits
and Basho to the frogs.

This is my home
my haven from the big city
and the babble of voices.
My home where I spend
idyllic weekends by the river
rolling around in Class B laughter
and smoking Franklins Mild.
My home where I watch
moths laying siege to storm lamps
singeing their wings on joss sticks
reincarnating on candles.

All roads lead
from the past to the future
from the suburbs to the epicentre
and Llandegley is as quiet
as Llandegley International Airport.

The air-space
above the old caravan site
is home to magpies and rooks
and migrant birds touching down
from transatlantic flights.

Across the green neighbourhood
animals that always remind me of Westerns
look at me with big eyes, big mouths chewing
cow parsley and grass.

Over the hedge
the road leads to Old Radnor
while the river runs its course joyfully
like a child going home for tea.

Was it here
I read *Born in Tibet*
was it here
I got homesick for my hometown
where I've spent the intervening years
sitting in my father's armchair
writing the minutes
of the river's soothing monologue
into my notebook.

Adam Flint

Valence

for Valerie Eales

A tarrier in the tumbled cuttings early sunlight warms
wants to fix its linger
ignore the fingers white clowns wag
tailor its shape to the shorn
sunday morning drunken parks
wherever silence perched
concentrate
young sap and marrow
ferment though a fatal term

*

Bruised wings flew black celldrunk echoes
over northern daylight tufts
slight webs
spotwhit
spunleaf edges
mercurial dog in dock
remedial re common nettle
yellow archangel
hop

*

to weak hook awake to white
regions and timid symmetry

deer-grass quave in the easterness
engrained a blexter

snagged dusk clouds down
closed and flush-jambed doors

*

Moledawn
sunnel
golden/taupe gloss

all well in afternoon augusts
piling husks north of the crags
in corners of open boyforts

dirtwarm thornlike
patches of process

*

A hardly discernible stigma wakes

capsules of yellow rattle by

chitin-scales grazed opaque

buckled highland fern

*

(In spundown margins then eventuals
the imagined mother wrings
hands over fragile thought)
black brook meniscus
pure-glint context
ripple mint + juxt
hilt-deep in white horehound

Up raw milkroots supple pillars rocket
into the evening's granular light
berries rust beneath the young
in October spikenard
                              shoot-heart
folded in raintide
boatsmile   a leaf
turned down at the margins
captains   48hrs

*

For two days four-fifths a taper
flits over sparse turf sprung plum limbs
moss walls thatch-ricks
the ventured-blind abounding with

encounters encounters
behind a facial cone

branchshine and pictures
auburn citrus
pinebread
milkpots
sitting around on grass-stems lightships stalk

*

One white clown cell sidles through the flush nodes
keeping healing blood from harm

like a minor fauna
into dottings semilunar
calamint and clary
light sleepers reaping pinlight
clinks on the lawn

Please help
Please help me
find and know a name enough to generate the face

elese we are only

offspring

of wordshape

*

Every breath a grey sac
dissembling through the dark
a secretive eluder skulking foodplant

beyond bound chambers
ditchborn screams
bush-hidden
scar-glittered
windows in knapweed
patched with neural tatting

*

Shadow-tailors threading
unbolted eaves to rust-eaten eyes
widened in outhouse subsidence

sang the epiphanies tabbies retire to
deep in crannied granary walls
never once in excess of the broad
shining median oblique darkness cuts
burrowing into the high barn rafters hollow knots

abandonment-embracers clone and

mother

their own wings

Claire Nashar

The Fish [edited]

wade [this question]
through[, and back with] black [proceed, drop] jade.
Of the crow-blue [stirs, the] mussel-shells, [and burn seeds] one keeps
adjusting [an order of the visible] the ash-heaps;
opening and shutting [divisibility] itself like [i know]

an
injured [future] fan[s us
keeps] The barnacles [kind] which encrust the [same] side
of the [same] wave, [a throat] cannot hide
there [much less tongue] for the submerged shafts [voice-lit] of the

sun [and ideal],
split like [you are] spun
[and the] glass [within], move[, underlight] themselves with spotlight
swiftness
[quivering] into the crevices [skinny]—
in and out, illuminating

the [silt of]
turquoise sea [and
curl] of bodies. The water [presses flowers] drives [weed] a wedge
of iron [air] through the iron [sky top] edge
of the cliff; whereupon the [emptied of] stars,

pink [silver
our love] rice-[pale in] grains [my love], ink-[sunk since
or] bespattered [eyes where] jelly fish, crabs [die] like green
[sick and then] lilies, and submarine [you are
with spore-filled] toadstools, slide each [in so] on the other [you

] All
external [Rock
marks [are marks least] of abuse [most] are present on this [float]
defiant edifice—
[its] all [toward a state] the physical features of [my ball fisted]

ac-
cident—lack [the story]
of cornice, dynamite [of astral aspect and] grooves, burns, and
hatchet strokes, these [claims masked] things [with] stand
out on it; the chasm [lung no]-side is

dead.
Repeated [water
is] evidence has proved [kinful,] that it can live[.
Put] on what can not revive
its youth. The sea grows old in [fussing] it

Eduardo Moga

translated by Terence Dooley

[Eyes Adhere to the Bodies]

Eyes adhere to bodies, they cede to their rigour and their clay. They lose whatever made them eyes, and yet they see more clearly, with more hands, more iron, more irony, like magnetised moons. Eyes, birds in a storm, are raised to other surfaces, and see within the seen. They isolate the bodies then, they wrap them up as if in gusts of winds that disappear into their own vortices, extract the brilliance of their dreams, the substance of their cloth, their sounding ruins, what they keep of bodies born to die.

The flow of gulls. The pavement is a cry. (To cry out is to age, as to caress). Cars drink the space.

(A black man passes by, I listen to his skin of water, skin of reeds. It whispers like silver. I hear the pain revealed in his sandals, his dusty glance, I hear the white extension of his silence, within it alkaloids and night. His every part: sphincter, lashes, fear, all told in his tense blood, in the elastic oneness of his blood beneath an aura of acacias and handkerchiefs).

Bodies carry with them ugliness or gift. My arms are theirs, their death is mine. Their roll towards repentance drags me down. My nipples, and navel, and inches, and vertical blood, and joints that sketch vague smiles, the rigging of my body brothers me to all the other bodies. In them lives what I have never been, flowers decapitated by distance, the noise eyes make, solidities that other lips have kissed, smouldering smiles, flames in whose waters I bathe, swamp-crystals of consciousness. Shapes that absorb the past and all that never came to exist.

(A lifeless someone passes by. Collar and tie. He doesn't know he decays. I note his yellow crown, his incogitant capillaries. Yet I need the odour of his evanescence, the brief infinitude that keeps him with us still, brief petiole).

Such longing to become the thing I see, to lodge in difference, to cross the threshold of the eye, to breathe through it, to light the dark spark, the stump of harmony.

I struggle with myself, my walls bite. I pay my skin no mind, it lays me siege. I fell the tree I am, it flees and hides in all its rectitude, and from its crown the birds fly up. To break out of one's skin, tear off the bark of breath, to make myself into someone outside myself, within the shining dark that covers every tomb and attitude. To glide like gulls along the edge of day, along the paper's blade, to be more, ambiguously more, but in the river of the new, in which qne body breathes made up of all the bodies.

(An inspecific someone passes by. He smells of birth, of nothingness; he shifts like me the weight of slavery. Another blow whose force is stifled in this polystyrene street. Another way of facing up to death).

The houses also move. Doves and geraniums breathe. The colours altered by the sun protest. Would I be them, the multiplicity that lives inside them, or the soft sky alien in its quietude? Would I be the silent washing hung to dry, or music of the unseen?

(Something goes by, an imaginary dog, a shape, a light, and in its lines I recognise the tongue I aspire to, the sons forgotten, standing on the back of time, the eyes, the birds, the symbols that draw breath, the names of all the nameless beings, these that loom about me like a body or a flood).

[I Walk Through Town...]

I walk through town. I watch its void
curdle on the tarmac,
tighten like a dawn
                 red
with fear, and it adorns the churches
and the brothels,
and gives no counsel, and stutters.
The sulphur I am
floats in this nothing, the silence I am,
the stench of death from
dark
gulls,
       whose mew
pierces the day
like shadow-darts. I watch the gulls,
and dogs who look like men, and men
who look like me,
who neglect to breathe, who misspend
their skin,
and mortgage their semen
and practise
futile
     habits:
being born,
learning to talk,
falling in love. And I watch
the rain: the abrasive
oneness of water
goading the earth,
and the sun sunk in a cacophony
of nos,
and my stolen eyes
and what lives in them:
                    the estranged,
the inert, the wingless,
eyes that shelter

dead light. No-one walks the streets, and yet
people
ejaculate, grow old, grow
resigned to their limbs, don't give up on life;
by no means,
they lend themselves to
promiscuity and dust:
they celebrate their agony;
and the outrage of their being
resounds in the caverns
of my body.
The street is empty, but provides me with
forms
I dissolve in,
chokes me with the breath
of the many, dazzles me with blackness
and desire.
The buses have warm
mouths,
no river ever flows through them,
not even
the chance of a river,
nor any
flying thing. And the blue
seeps into what isn't blue,
transfuses
its blood, queers it
with its chisel, enslaves its bruised glass.
A breast
lays me siege:
It is my own. Other breasts
offer their healing balm,
but I slide down their sides
and stammer, and am mirrored
in their insistent lacquer,
and hardly notice when they call
my names, enumerate
my deaths, and see me with my eyes,

from inside me. I am not here.
I cannot feel the ribs surrounding me.
I won't take part in the luminosity
with which
things soil themselves,
that embraces me
unwillingly, as if to fend me off.
I pay no mind to tongues, to chalices,
to landslides or to worlds.
In brief, I don't watch people making love,
or objects reproducing,
                                nor do I inhabit
the bustle of quietude, the daily life
of insects anointed
in the boreal yoke
of neon.
Now all I am
                is this limbless
wandering, this repeal
of the caress; it pours me down
a new abyss and offers me
its shredded pulp:
in its viscosities I itemise
smiling skulls
and their smiles.

Marie-Luise Kaschnitz

translated by Harry Guest

Europa

When on the New Year nightfall over a stricken world,
home of unrest, hate between brothers, insurrection, sin,
home of rash ideas, flaming speeches, loveliness –
When on the New Year nightfall bells ring out
raised again awkwardly into their shattered towers
those great bells –
When in a parched south wind flood-water laps at the bridges –
When trains re-whistle and foghorns moan once more –
When the strange voice calls Glad New Year to a silent window

A heart maybe drawn to the loved-one soundlessly whispers
Love me for ever, all through the days ahead

To be torn away by the bell-winds, the storm-winds
over familiar borders, over the distant town,
over lands that have nothing to say

Hear many prophecies and prayers ascending
to summon the day with peace in abundance,
when the righteous will flourish,
the lawless have fled, can' t be found where they'd been,
talk also of crops gone gold from the dead in their graves,
of gardens unwalled which bloom and bear fruit,
of a world so unique none will fear any more,
of a peacetime stretching for ever.

But also what Nostradamus foresaw long ago –
horses from Asia that drink in the Rhine,
a bloodbath to flow till the start of The Kingdom,
towns that collapse, fields laid waste till the start of The Kingdom,
armies of violence breaking from east and from west

rebounding like waves at spring-tide, brazen
and losing their way like the waves at spring-tide.
But where they have been is desolation.
Bees used to hum on the steppes they came over.
A no-man's-land now. Lost from the past.

And he, the dream-wanderer, paces away with the bell-winds, the
        storm-winds,
over a shivering section of world,
home for hate between brothers, insurrection, sin,
home for rash ideas, flaming speeches, loveliness.
He touches once more the coast of Brittany,
where laurel and roses writhe in Atlantic gales,
as far as the sea round the Golden Horn,
from Midgard, home of the living,
as far as the Pillars of Hercules.

And a shape from the past presses towards him, clumsy ghouls
        from the Alps,
maidens winged like a swan, the black steed of Poseidon,
castles he sees, temples and cloisters, vaulting, palaces,
and always a ploughman on autumn fields, and over and over again
troops on the march, all armed.

And voices clang up to him, choirs of passion
yearning for pleasure and longing for love and ever
again the detailed defiant and grimly forsaken
voice of Prometheus.

But then all grows quieter.
Noiseless in moonlight and under tattered clouds
a sweetness prospers towards him, untroubled –
marble joy in Vicenza, fountains spurting in Rome,
crazy girls flirting by the Minster in Freiburg,
rose-windows of Chartres and Goethe's garden flanked by a star.

And he thinks he's never encountered such splendour, such fullness
        of promise,

his eyes seeming brighter than those of a man who guards
      graveyards,
his hands seeming stronger than those of a man who guards
      graveyards,
his own heart filled with the thrill of existence.

And he's forced to cry out, to the world, plead for certainty
that without the consent of peace
    without the consent of those who come after us
        nothing must be suppressed, nothing wiped out
        not bliss in a gaze
        freedom of the soul
        lift in the heart
        nor from the tower the old sound
        of the watchman's solitary voice.

Though he shouts, the dream-wanderer, shouts in to the world
no answer rings back to him. Only the bells
singing of storm, singing of liberty,
singing of death, singing of Christmas,
those mysterious bells no-one can decipher
carry on calling
in the depths of the night.

Yet, when he turns home dejected, drawn there again,
and whispers afresh his *Love me each day*
the heart in his heart passed the year long ago
patiently able to cope with each
tiny repetitive setback.

Translator's Note
Jahrhundertmitte [Mid-Century], an anthology published by Insel Verlag,
Frankfurt, in 1955 – in which this poem appeared – only contained poems
written after 1945 because they looked both to the appalling past and the
incalculable future. This poem expresses the confusion of those times seen
by an unorthodox Christian who has lived through what has occurred and
is bewildered by what may be achieved as remedy and restoration.

Günter Eich

translated by Ken Cockburn

§

The gardener seeds a lawn among tares,
plants a bed of phlox by the wall.
In my room the cobwebs have all been swept away
so time doesn't snag there.

Just let go of them: Bellum Gallicum,
Rembrandt, soup kitchens, artichokes in Bern,
sea-views and graves –

lawn, tares and phlox,
sown together with hopes
for cobwebs and laughter,
for the world's unpainted pictures.

§

May doesn't stay for long,
seven eight nine minutes,
an immaterial blink of the eye
with light rain and a southerly breeze,

one might ask it nicely to come again,
as if it mattered,
one might ask it nicely to stay,
as if it mattered.

§

Only dimming.
If the neighbours knock –
with legs drawn up
in the window-recess,
one more look
at the useless bed
and the daily resolutions,
ready to lay down the weight outside
where between snowflakes
twilight falls on the grass,
no clear ending,
a possibility,
dimming.

§

1.11.68 for Ilse

Cutty Sark,
a long-
standing theme,
neither crucial
nor without surprises –
but now relinquished:
Greenwich and etymology,
a Scottish legend, Hart Crane
– today we're able to drink it
and rediscover its mysteriousness.
From the fact there are
made-up mysteries
we'll take consolation:
tracing one theme
while the outlines
of others
remain hidden.

Fumbling for Words

The first words
for leaves and rushes,
found in a clearing
on untrodden snow,

pocketed
in threadbare trousers,
lost on a streetcar
at the age of fifteen.

§

Cartographies

This world,
so simple in atlases:
inlets and islands,
brown, green or blue,
the apparent order
of circumscribed towns,
carefree and deathless.

This world, this winter,
these shipping routes,
we want to trace them
meticulously.
That's where it'll be.
There,
a clue.

Notes on Contributors

NB. Work by Lucy Hamilton, Sabiyha Rasheed and Peter Riley has been repeated from the last issue, as they were affected by misprints and we felt that these were bad enough to warrant re-presentation here in their correct form. Our apologies to all concerned. Later printings of the last issue were correct, but the first run of subscriber copies was not.

LIZ ADAMS is a poet whose work has appeared in *Stand, Ghosts of Gone Birds (Bloomsbury), Shadowtrain, The Frogmore Papers, morphrog #NewWriting*, amongst others. She has MA in Creative Writing from the University of East Anglia and an MRes in Humanities and Cultural Studies from the London Consortium. Her first book of poems, *Green Dobermans*, was published in 2011. She lives in Exeter where she co-hosts Uncut Poets.

CLARK ALLISON lives in Scotland. This is his first appearance in the magazine.

ANNABEL BANKS teaches at the University of Falmouth. She works in both poetry and prose, and won both of Cambridge University's creative writing prizes, the Ryan Kinsella Poetry Prize and the RSC "Other" Prize for theatre. In 2015 she received three nominations for the Pushcart Prize, a nomination for the Queen's Ferry Press *Best Short Fictions 2016*, and a further nomination for Blazevox's *Bettering American Poetry*.

KEN COCKBURN is a Scottish poet and translator, based in Edinburgh. In 2014, Shearsman published his book *the road north*, which he co-authored with Alec Finlay.

JOEY CONNOLLY lives in London, where he edits *Kaffeeklatsch* and manages the annual Free Verse Poetry Book Fair. He received an Eric Gregory Award in 2012, and his first collection will appear from Carcanet in 2016.

SUSAN CONNOLLY lives in Drogheda, Ireland. Shearsman published her second collection, *Forest Music* (2009), as well as a chapbook of visual poems, *The Sun-Artist* (2013), and will follow this with a full-length collection of visual work, *Bridge of the Ford*, this year.

MAKYLA CURTIS is currently studying at the University of Auckland. Her work has previously appeared in a number of New Zealand publications (Blackmail press, *REM Magazine, Rejectamenta*), and she is also an editor for *Potroast 'Zine* (www.potroast.co.nz), an Auckland-based experimental writing and visual-media magazine.

ADAM DAY is the author of *Model of a City in Civil War* (Sarabande Books), as well as the recipient of a 2010 Poetry Society of America Chapbook Fellowship for *Badger, Apocrypha*, and of a 2011 PEN Emerging Writers Award. He also directs the Baltic Writing Residency in Latvia, Scotland, and Bernheim Forest.

TERENCE DOOLEY lives in London, and is translating a *Selected Poems* by Eduardo Moga for Shearsman Books.

GÜNTER EICH (1907-1972) was one of the most important post-war German poets, and a founder member of the *Gruppe 47*. His collected poems (*Sämtliche Gedichte*) are available from Suhrkamp Verlag, Berlin, in 2 volumes. He was also a prolific writer of radio plays. The first substantial collection of his work in English appeared in 2010, translated by Michael Hoffmann under the title *Angina Days* (Princeton University Press).

ADAM FLINT was born in North London and lives in Berlin. Previous poems have been published in/by *Critical Documents, Stand, The Journal, The Rialto* and *Sand* (Berlin), among others.

HARRY GUEST's complete poetic output is available from Anvil Press Poetry in the form of *A Puzzling Harvest: Collected Poems 1955-2000* (2002), and *Some Times* (2010). Shearsman published one book *hors de série* in 2008, *Comparisons & Conversions* – a long poem and some uncollected translations – and will publish another volume of his translations, *Otherlands*, in 2016. His next poetry collection will appear from Shearsman in 2017.

LUCY HAMILTON co-edits *Long Poem Magazine* and teaches freelance. Her collection *Stalker* (Shearsman, 2012) was shortlisted for the Forward Prizes' Felix Dennis Prize for Best First Collection. In a recent commissioned project, poems from the 'Diarists' sequence were exhibited at the The Scott Polar Museum, Cambridge, and also appeared in *PN Review*. Other poems from her second collection-in-progress have appeared in *Shearsman, PN Review, Tears in the Fence, Molly Bloom* and *Litmus*.

JULI JANA's chapbook *r-at* was published by Shearsman in 2014. An artist and poet originally from South Africa, she lives in London.

NORMAN JOPE lives in Plymouth. He is the author of several collections, including *Dreams of the Caucasus* (Shearsman Books. 2010).

MARIE-LUISE KASCHNITZ (1901-1974) was a leading figure in post-war German literature. As well as poetry, she wrote essays, novels and short stories, and won the Georg Büchner Prize in 1955. A selected volume of her poems, *Gedichte*, remains in print at Suhrkamp Verlag, Berlin, as do some collections of her short stories.

LINDA KEMP is based in Sheffield. Recent work has appeared in *Blackbox Manifold, e-ratio, Lighthouse, M58* and in two pamphlets, *Immunological* and *Blueprint*, published by enjoy your homes press.

KENNY KNIGHT lives in Plymouth. Shearsman Books published his first collection, *The Honicknowle Book of the Dead*, in 2009.

EDUARDO MOGA is originally from Barcelona, but currently lives in London. A bilingual selected is in development here at Shearsman Books. His most recent publication consists of a year's worth of blog entries documenting his first year in London after moving from Spain: *Corónicas de Ingalaterra* (Ediciones de la Isla de Siltola, 2015). Recent poetry collections include *El corazón, la nada* (Eds. Amargord, 2014) and *Insumisión* (Vaso Roto, 2013). In 2016 he was named Director of the Editora Regional de Extremadura.

CLARE NASHAR is an Australian poet currently living and studying in Buffalo, NY.

ALASDAIR PATERSON's two most recent collections are *on the governing of empires* (2010) and *Elsewhere or Thereabouts* (2014), both from Shearsman.

SIMON PERCHIK has been appearing in this magazine since its very earliest run back in 1981-2. He lives in Long Island, NY, and has published many collections of poetry, including a collected edition, *Hands Collected* (Pavement Saw Press, 2000)

SABIYHA RASHEED is a recent graduate from the University of Kent with a degree in English and American Literature with Creative Writing. Sabiyha is a singer-songwriter and her involvement in the arts, both with music and literature, has aided her exploration of poetry. She is continuing with a collection of poetry, focusing on her interest in race politics and will be published in the University of Kent's 50th Anniversary Anthology.

YVONNE REDDICK is a Research Fellow at the University of Central Lancashire, and is Visiting Fellow at the Centre for the Study of International Slavery, University of Liverpool. She has a poetry pamphlet, *Deerhart*, being published this year by Knives, Forks and Spoons Press.

PETER RILEY was born into an environment of working people in the Manchester area in 1940 and now lives in retirement in Hebden Bridge, West Yorkshire. His most recent books are *The Glacial Stairway* (Carcanet Press, 2011) and *Due North* (Shearsman Books, 2015), a book-length poem which was shortlisted for the Forward Prize for Best Collection, 2015. He regularly contributes reviews of new poetry to the website *The Fortnightly Review*, and a collection of these was issued in book form by under the title *The Fortnightly Reviews 2012-2014.*

DAVID RUSHMER lives in Cambridge, where he works as a librarian at the University; his publications include *Blanchot's Ghost* (Oystercatcher Press 2008).

ALEXANDRA SASHE, originally from Russia, now lives in Vienna. Her first collection, *Antibodies*, was published by Shearsman Books in 2013.

MATTHEW STOPPARD lives in Leeds, where he is a librarian. He has two collections from Valley Press, *A Family Behind Glass* (2013) and *Cinema Stories*, the latter jointly authored with James Nash (2015).

ALAN WALL is a professor at the University of Chester. His many publications include 8 novels, most recently *Badmouth* (Harbour Books, 2014), and 4 poetry collections from Shearsman, the most recent of which is *Endtimes* (2013).

www.ingramcontent.com/pod-product-compliance
Lightning Source LLC
Chambersburg PA
CBHW030957090426
42737CB00007B/578